Pythagoras And The Temple Of Delphi

Edouard Schure

Kessinger Publishing's Rare Reprints

Thousands of Scarce and Hard-to-Find Books on These and other Subjects!

- Americana
- Ancient Mysteries
- Animals
- Anthropology
- Architecture
- Arts
- Astrology
- Bibliographies
- Biographies & Memoirs
- Body, Mind & Spirit
- Business & Investing
- Children & Young Adult
- Collectibles
- Comparative Religions
- Crafts & Hobbies
- Earth Sciences
- Education
- Ephemera
- Fiction
- Folklore
- Geography
- Health & Diet
- History
- Hobbies & Leisure
- Humor
- Illustrated Books
- Language & Culture
- Law
- Life Sciences
- Literature
- Medicine & Pharmacy
- Metaphysical
- Music
- Mystery & Crime
- Mythology
- Natural History
- Outdoor & Nature
- Philosophy
- Poetry
- Political Science
- Science
- Psychiatry & Psychology
- Reference
- Religion & Spiritualism
- Rhetoric
- Sacred Books
- Science Fiction
- Science & Technology
- Self-Help
- Social Sciences
- Symbolism
- Theatre & Drama
- Theology
- Travel & Explorations
- War & Military
- Women
- Yoga
- *Plus Much More!*

We kindly invite you to view our catalog list at:
http://www.kessinger.net

CHAPTER III

THE TEMPLE OF DELPHI—THE SCIENCE OF
APOLLO—THEORY OF DIVINATION—THE
PYTHONESS THEOCLEA

FROM the plain of Phocis the traveller mounts the
smiling meadows bordering the banks of the
Pleistus to plunge into a winding valley shut in
between lofty mountains. At every step the way
becomes narrower and the country more sublime and
deserted. Finally a circle of rugged mountains,
crowned with wild-looking peaks, a veritable store-
house of electricity, over which storms often raged,
is reached. Suddenly, far up the sombre gorge
appears the town of Delphi, like an eagle's nest, on
a rock surrounded by precipices and dominated by
the two peaks of Parnassus. From the distance the
bronze Victories are seen sparkling in the light, as
well as the brazen horses, the innumerable statues
of gold, marshalled along the sacred path and
arranged like a guard of heroes and gods round the
Doric temple of Phœbus Apollo.

This was the most sacred spot in Greece. Here,

the Pythoness prophesied and the Amphictyons assembled; here, the different Hellenic peoples had built round the sanctuary chapels containing treasured offerings. Here, processions of men, women, and children, coming from afar, mounted the sacred path to greet the God of Light. From time immemorial religion had consecrated Delphi to the veneration of the people. Its central situation in Hellas, its rock sheltered from profane hands and easy to defend, had contributed to this result. The place was calculated to strike the imagination, for a singular quality gave it great prestige. In a cavern behind the temple was a cleft in the rock from which issued a cold, vapoury mist, inducing, it was said, a state of inspiration and ecstasy. Plutarch relates that in by-gone times a shepherd, when seated by the side of this cleft, began to prophesy. At first he was looked upon as mad, but when his predictions became realized, people began to investigate. The priests took possession of the spot and consecrated it to the divinity. Hence the institution of the Pythoness, who was seated above the cleft on a tripod. The vapours exhaling from the abyss occasioned convulsions and strange crises, provoking in her that *second sight* noticed in certain somnambulists. Eschylus, whose affirmation is not without weight, for he was the son of a priest of

3

Eleusis, and an initiate himself, tells us in his *Eumenides*, by the mouth of the Pythoness, that Delphi had first been consecrated to the Earth, then to Themis (Justice), afterwards to Phœbe (the interceding moon), and finally to Apollo, the solar god. In temple symbolism each of these names represents long periods, and embraces centuries of time. The fame of Delphi, however, dates from Apollo. Jupiter, according to the poets, wishing to find the centre of the earth, started two eagles in their flight from east and west, and they met at Delphi. Whence comes this prestige, this world-wide and unchallenged authority which constituted Apollo as the god of Greece *par excellence*, and now makes the glory of his name inexplicable to us?

History is dumb on this important point. Question orators, poets, and philosophers, they will only give you superficial explanations. The real answer to this question remained the secret of the temple. Let us try to fathom it.

In Orphic thought, Dionysos and Apollo were two different revelations of the same divinity. Dionysos represented esoteric truth, the foundation and interior of things, open to initiates alone. He held the mysteries of life, past and future existences, the relations between soul and body, heaven and earth. Apollo personified the same truth applied to life on earth and social order. The inspirer of poetry, medicine, and laws, he was science by divination, beauty by art, peace among nations by justice, and harmony between soul and body by purification. In a word, to the initiate Dionysos signified nothing less than the divine spirit in evolution in the universe; and Apollo, the manifestation thereof to mankind on earth. The people had been made to understand this by a legend. The priests had told them that, in the time of Orpheus, Bacchus and Apollo had vied with one another for the tripod of Delphi. Bacchus had willingly given it up to his brother, and withdrawn to one of the peaks of Parnassus, where the Theban women were wont to celebrate his mysteries. In reality the two sons of Jupiter divided between themselves the empire of the world. The one reigned over the mysterious Beyond, the other over the World of the Living.

So that we find in Apollo the solar Logos, the universal Word, the mighty Mediator, the Vishnu of the Hindus, the Mithras of the Persians, and the Horus of the Egyptians. The old ideas of Asiatic esoterism, however, took on, in the legend of Apollo, a plastic beauty, and an incisive splendour which made them penetrate the more deeply into human consciousness, like the shafts of the God.

" White-winged serpents springing forth from his golden bow," says Eschylus.

Apollo springs forth from the mighty night at Delos; all the goddesses greet his birth; he walks and takes up his bow and lyre, his locks stream in the air and his quiver rattles on his shoulder; the sea quivers, and the whole island shines with his glory scattered abroad in floods of golden flame. This is the epiphany of divine light, which by its august presence creates order, splendour, and harmony, of which poetry is the marvellous echo. The god goes to Delphi and pierces with his arrows a monstrous serpent which was ravaging and laying waste the land, he purifies the country and establishes the Temple; the image of the victory of this divine light over darkness and evil. In ancient religions, the serpent symbolized at once the fatal circle of life and the evil resulting therefrom. And yet, from this life once understood and overcome, springs forth knowledge. Apollo, slayer of the serpent, is the symbol of the initiate who pierces nature by science, tames it by his will, and breaking the Karmic circle of the flesh mounts aloft in spiritual splendour, whilst the broken fragments of human animality lie writhing in the sand. For this reason Apollo is the master of expiation, of the purification of soul and body. Bespattered with

the monster's blood, he performed expiation, puri-
fied himself during an eight years' exile beneath the
bitter, health-giving laurels of the vale of Tempe.—
Apollo, trainer of men, likes to take up his abode
in their midst, he is pleased to be in towns with the
youths and young men, at contests of poetry and
the palaestra, though he remains only for a time.
In autumn he returns to his own land, the home of
the Hyperboreans. This is the mysterious people
of luminous and transparent souls who dwell in the
eternal dawn of perfect felicity. Here are his true
priests, his beloved priestesses. He lives with them
in strong, intimate communion, and when he wishes
to make mankind a royal gift, he brings back from
the country of the Hyperboreans one of those
mighty, radiant souls who is born on earth to teach
and delight mortals. He himself returns to Delphi
every spring, when poems and hymns are sung in
his honour. Visible to none but initiates he comes
in dazzling Hyperborean glory, in a chariot drawn
by sweetly-singing swans. Again he takes up his
abode in the sanctuary, where the Pythoness speaks
forth his oracles, and sages and poets listen. Then
is heard the song of nightingales, the fountain of
Castalia scatters silver spray on every hand,
dazzling light and celestial music penetrate the
heart of man and reach the very veins of nature.

In this legend of the Hyperboreans may be found much light thrown on the esoteric basis of the Apollo myth. The land of the Hyperboreans is the Beyond, the empyrean of victorious souls, whose astral dawns light up its many-coloured zones. Apollo himself personifies the immaterial and intelligible light of which the sun is merely the physical image, and from which flows down all truth. The wonderful swans which bring him are poets and divine geniuses, messengers of his mighty solar soul, leaving behind them flashes of light and strains of glorious music. Hyperborean Apollo, accordingly, personifies the descent of heaven on to earth, the incarnation of spiritual beauty in flesh and blood, the inflow of transcendent truth by inspiration and divination.

It is now the moment to raise the golden veil of legend and enter the temple itself. How was divination practised therein? Here we touch upon the secrets of Apollonian science and of the mysteries of Delphi.

In antiquity, a strong tie united divination to the solar cults, and here we have the golden key to all the so-called magic mysteries.

The worship of Aryan humanity from the beginning of civilization was directed towards the sun as the source of light, heat, and life. When, how-

ever, the thought of the sages rose from the phenomenon to the cause, behind this sensible fire, this
visible light, they formed the concept of an immaterial fire, an intelligible light. They identified
the form with the male principle, the creative spirit
or intellectual essence of the universe, and the latter
with its female principle, its formative soul, its
plastic substance. This intuition dates back to time
immemorial. The conception I speak of is con-
nected with the most ancient mythologies. It circulates in the Vedic hymns under the form of Agni,
the universal fire which penetrates all things. It
blossoms forth in the religion of Zoroaster, the esoteric part of which is represented by the cult of
Mithras. Mithras is the male fire and Mitra the
female light. Zoroaster formally states that the
Eternal, by means of the living Word, created the
heavenly light, the seed of Ormuzd, the principle of
material light and material fire. For the initiate of
Mithras the sun is only a rude reflection of this
light. In his obscure grotto, whose vault is painted
with stars, he invokes the sun of grace, the fire of
love, conqueror of evil, reconciler of Ormuzd and
Ahriman, purifier and mediator, who dwells in the
soul of the holy prophets. In the crypts of Egypt,
the initiates seek this same sun under the name of
Osiris. When Hermes asks to be allowed to con-

template the origin of things, at first he feels himself plunged into the ethereal waves of a delicious light, in which move all living forms. Then, plunging into the darkness of dense matter, he hears a voice which he recognizes as *the voice of light*. At the same time fire darts forth from the depths, immediately all is light and chaos becomes order. In the *Book of the Dead* of the Egyptians the souls journey painfully towards that light in the barque of Isis. Moses fully adopted this doctrine in Genesis: "Elohim said: Let there be light; and there was light." Now the creation of this light precedes that of the sun and stars. This means that, in the order of principles and cosmogony, intelligible precedes material light. The Greeks, who moulded into human form and dramatized the most abstract ideas, expressed the same doctrine in the myth of Hyperborean Apollo.

Consequently the human mind, by inner contemplation of the universe, from the point of view of the soul and the intelligence, came to conceive of an intelligible light, an imponderable element serving as an intermediary between matter and spirit. It would be easy to show that natural philosophers of modern times insensibly draw somewhere near the same conclusion along an opposite path, *i. e.* by searching for the constitution of matter and seeing

the impossibility of explaining it by itself. Even in
the sixteenth century, Paracelsus, whilst studying
the chemical combinations and metamorphoses of
bodies, went so far as to admit of a universal occult
agent by means of which they are brought about.
The natural philosophers of the sixteenth and seven-
teenth centuries, who conceived of the universe as
being a dead machine, believed in the absolute void
of celestial space. Yet when it was discovered that
light is not the emission of a radiant matter, but
rather the vibration of an imponderable element,
one was obliged to admit that the whole of space is
filled by an infinitely subtile fluid penetrating all
bodies and through which waves of heat and light
are transmitted.   Thus a return was made to the
Greek ideas of natural philosophy and theosophy.
Newton, who had spent his whole life in studying
the movements of the heavenly bodies, went even
farther than this. He called this ether *sensorium
Dei,* or the brain of God, *i. e.* the organ by which
divine thought acts in the infinitely great as well
as in the infinitely small.   In emitting this idea,
which he regarded as necessary to explain the
simple rotation of the heavenly bodies, the great
natural philosopher had embarked on the open
sea of esoteric philosophy.   The very ether Newton's thought found in space Paracelsus had dis-

alembic
The alchemist's flask

covered at the bottom of his alembics, and had named it astral light. Now this imponderable fluid, which is everywhere present, penetrating all things, this subtile but indispensable agent, this light, invisible to our eyes, but which is at the bottom of all phosphorescence and scintillation, has been proved to exist by a German natural philosopher in a series of well-appointed experiments. Reichenbach had noticed that subjects of very sensitive nerve fibre, when placed in a perfectly dark room in front of a magnet, saw at its two ends strong rays of red, yellow, and blue light. Sometimes these rays vibrated with an undulatory movement. He continued his experiments with all kinds of bodies, especially with crystals. Luminous emanations were seen, by sensitive subjects, round all these bodies. Around the heads of men placed in the dark room they saw white rays; from their fingers issued small flames. In the first portion of their sleep somnambulists sometimes see their magnetizer with these same signs. Pure astral light appears only in a condition of lofty ecstasy, but it is polarized in all bodies, combines with all terrestrial fluids and plays diverse *rôles* in electricity, in terrestrial and animal magnetism.[1] The

[1] Reichenbach called this fluid *odyle*. His work has been translated into English by Gregory: *Researches on Magnetism, Electricity, Heat, Light, Cristalization and Chemical Attraction.*—London, 1850.

interest of Reichenbach's experiments is that they make precise the limits and transition from physical to astral vision capable of leading on to spiritual vision. They also enable us to obtain a faint glimpse of the infinite subtilties of imponderable matter. Along this path there is nothing to prevent our conceiving it as so fluid, so subtile and penetrating, that it becomes in some way homogeneous with spirit, serving the latter as a perfect garment.

We have just seen that modern natural philosophy, in order to explain the world, has been obliged to recognize an imponderable, universal agent, that it has even proved its presence, and, in this way, without knowing it, has fallen in with the notions of ancient theosophies. Let us now try to define the nature and function of cosmic fluid in accordance with the philosophy of occultism in all ages. On this main principle of cosmogony, Zoroaster is in agreement with Heraclitus, Pythagoras with Saint Paul, the Kabbalists with Paracelsus. Cybele-Maïa reigns everywhere, the mighty soul of the world, the vibrating and plastic substance which the breath of the creative spirit uses at its will. Her oceans of ether serve to cement together all the worlds. She is the great mediator between the invisible and the visible, between spirit and matter,

between the within and the without of the universe.
Condensed in enormous masses in the atmosphere
beneath the action of the sun, she flashes forth in a
thunderbolt.   Absorbed by the earth she circulates
in magnetic currents.   Subtilized in the nervous
system of the animal she transmits her will to the
limbs, her sensations to the brain.   More than that,
this subtile fluid forms living organisms similar to
material bodies.   It serves as substance to the astral
body of the soul, a garment of light which the spirit
is ever weaving for itself.   The fluid becomes transformed, it rarefies or densifies according to the souls
it clothes or the worlds it envelops.   Not only does
it embody spirit and spiritualize matter in its living
bosom, it reflects in a perpetual mirage both things
and the thoughts and wills of mankind.   The
strength and duration of these images is in proportion to the intensity of the will producing them.
And, in truth, there is no other means of explaining
thought suggestion and transmission at a distance,
that principle of magic now-a-days acknowledged
and recognized by science.[1]   Thus in the astral
light the past of the worlds trembles in vague
images, and the future is there also, with the living

---

[1] See the Bulletin of the Société de Pyschologie Physiologique.   M.
Charcot, president, 1885.   See more especially the fine book by M.
Ochorowicz, *De la Suggestion Mentale*, Paris, 1887.

souls inevitably destined to descend into flesh. This is the meaning of the veil of Isis and the mantle of Cybele, into which all beings are woven.

It is now seen that the theosophical doctrine of the astral light is identical with the secret doctrine of the solar Word in the religions of Greece and the East. It is also seen how closely allied this doctrine is to that of divination. The astral light is there revealed as the universal medium of the phenomena of vision and of ecstasy which it explains. It is at once the vehicle which transmits the movements of thought, and the living mirror in which the soul contemplates the images of the material and spiritual world. Once transported into this element, the spirit of the seer leaves corporeal conditions. For him the measure of time and space is changed. In some way he participates in the ubiquity of the universal fluid. For him opaque matter becomes transparent, and the soul, disengaging itself from the body and rising in its own light, penetrates, in a state of ecstasy, into the spiritual world, sees souls clothed in their ethereal bodies and communicates with them. All the initiates of former times had a clear notion of this *second sight,* or direct spiritual vision. Witness Eschylus, who puts into the mouth of the shade of Clytemnestra :

"Look at these wounds, thy spirit can see them; when one is asleep, the spirit possesses a more piercing vision; in broad daylight, the eyes of mortals see but a little way."

Let me add that this theory of clairvoyance and ecstasy is in wonderful agreement with the numerous experiments, scientifically carried out by savants and doctors of modern times, on lucid somnambulists and clairvoyants of every kind.[1] From these contemporary facts I shall endeavour briefly to characterize the successive psychic conditions from simple clairvoyance to cataleptic ecstasy.

The state of clairvoyance, as is seen by thousands

[1] There is a great deal of literature on this subject, very unequal in value, in France, Germany and England. I will here mention two books in which the subject is treated scientifically by men of real worth.

(1) *Letters on Animal Magnetism*, by William Gregory, London, 1850. Gregory was a professor of chemistry at the University of Edinburgh. His book is a profound study of the phenomena of animal magnetism, from suggestion to vision at a distance and lucid clairvoyance, on subjects observed by himself, in accordance with scientific method, and with minute exactness.

(2) *Die mystischen Erscheinungen der menschlichen Natur*, von Maximilian Perty, Leipzig, 1872. Perty is a professor of philosophy and medicine at the University of Berne. His book presents an immense repertory of all such occult phenomena as have historical value. The extremely remarkable chapter on clairvoyance (Schlafwachen), Volume I., contains twenty accounts of female and five of male clairvoyants, related by the doctors who treated the cases. That of Weiner, treated by the author, is most curious. See also the treatises on magnetism by Dupotet and Deleuze, and the very strange book, *Die Seherin von Prévorst*, by Justinus Kerner.

of well-established facts, is a psychic one, differing as greatly from sleep as from a waking condition. The intellectual faculties of the clairvoyant, far from diminishing, increase in marvellous fashion. His memory is more correct, his imagination more active, his intelligence more alert. The main point, in a word, is that we have here developed a new sense, which is no longer corporeal, but rather belongs to the soul. Not only are the thoughts of the magnetizer transmitted to him as in the simple phenomenon of suggestion, which itself is outside the physical plane, but the clairvoyant even reads the thoughts of those present, sees through walls, penetrates hundreds of miles into homes where he has never been, and reads the private life of people he does not know. His eyes are closed, incapable of seeing anything, but his spirit sees farther and better than his open eyes and seems to travel about freely in space.[1] In a word, though clairvoyance may be abnormal from the bodily point of view, it is a normal and superior state from the point of view of the spirit. The consciousness has become deeper, the vision wider. The ego remains the same, but it has passed over to a higher plane, where the vision, freed from the coarse organs of the body, embraces

---

[1] Numerous examples in Gregory's work: Letters XVI, XVII, and XVIII.

and penetrates a vaster horizon.[1]   It is to be noted
that certain somnambulists, when submitting to the
passes of the magnetizer, feel themselves flooded
with increasingly dazzling light, whilst the awaking
seems to them an unpleasant return to darkness.

[1] The German philosopher, Schelling, has acknowledged the great
importance of somnambulism in the question of the immortality of the
soul.   He remarks that, in lucid sleep, there is produced an elevation
of the soul, and its relative liberation with regard to the body, which
does not take place in the normal state.   In somnambulists, everything
indicates the loftiest consciousness, as though their whole being were
met in one luminous focus, uniting together, past, present and future.
Far from losing all memory of the past, it lies open before them, and
even the veil of the future is at times cast aside in a glorious ray of
light.   If this is possible in earthly life, Schelling inquires, is it not
certain that our spiritual personality, which follows us in death, is at
this very moment present in us, that it is not born then but simply set
free, and shows itself when it is no longer bound by the senses to the
outside world?   The post-mortem condition is accordingly more real
than the earthly one.   For in this life, that which is accidental, ming-
ling with the whole, paralyzes in us that which is essential.   Schelling
calls the future state quite simply, clairvoyance.   The spirit liberated
from everything accidental in earthly life becomes stronger and more
alive; the wicked man becomes worse, the good better.

Quite recently Charles du Prel has advanced the same opinion,
supporting it with numerous facts and details in a well-written volume,
Philosophie der Mystik (1886).   He starts from this fact: the consciousness of the ego does not exhaust its object.   " Soul and consciousness are not two adequate terms; they do not cover one another as
they have not an equal scope.   The sphere of the soul far surpasses
that of the consciousness."   Consequently there is *a latent ego* in us.
This latent ego, which manifests itself in sleep and in dreams, is the real
ego, supra-terrestrial and transcendent, whose existence precedes our
terrestrial ego which is bound to the body.   The terrestrial ego is
perishable, the transcendent ego is immortal.   This is what St. Pau
meant when he said—"——the Lord Jesus Christ, who shall change
our vile body, so that it be fashioned like unto His glorious body."

Suggestion, thought reading, and distant vision are facts which already prove the independent existence of the soul, and transport us above the physical plane of the universe without making us leave it altogether. Clairvoyance, however, has infinite varieties and a scale of different states far wider than that of the waking condition. In proportion as the scale is mounted the phenomena become rarer and more extraordinary. I will mention only the principal stages. *Retrospection* is a vision of past events preserved in the astral light and revived by the sympathy of the seer. *Divination,* properly so called, is a problematical vision of things to come either by introspection of the thoughts of the living which contain future actions in germ, or by the occult influence of superior spirits which unfold the future in living images before the soul of the clairvoyant. In both cases they are projections of thoughts into the astral light. Finally *ecstasy* is defined as a vision of the spiritual world, where good or evil spirits appear to the seer in human form and communicate with him. The soul seems really to be transported out of the body, which life has almost left, and which stiffens into a state of catalepsy resembling death. From what those who have been in a condition of sublime ecstasy tell us, nothing in the universe can express

4

the beauty and splendour of these visions, or the sentiment of an ineffable fusion with the divine essence which they bring back, a very transport of light and music. The reality of these visions may be doubted. It must, nevertheless, be added that if the soul, in the average state of clairvoyance, has a correct perception of distant places and of absent ones, it is logical to admit that, in its loftiest exaltation, it may have the vision of a higher and an immaterial reality.

In my opinion, it will be the task of the future to restore to the transcendent faculties of the human soul their dignity and social function, by reorganizing them under the control of science and on the basis of a religion which is truly universal, open to all truths. Then science, regenerated by real faith and the spirit of love, will, with open eyes, mount aloft to those spheres in which speculative philosophy gropes about with bandaged eyes. Yes, science will become clear-sighted and redeeming in her mission, just in proportion as the consciousness and love of humanity increase in her. Perhaps it is through "the gate of sleep and dreams," as Homer said, that divine Psyche, banished from our civilized life and weeping in silence beneath her veil, will regain possession of her altars.

Anyhow, the phenomena of clairvoyance, studied

from every aspect by present-day savants and doctors, throw an altogether new light on the *rôle* of divination in antiquity and on a host of apparently supernatural phenomena, with which the annals of every nation and people are filled. Of course, a distinction must be made between legend and history, hallucination and real vision. Still, the experimental psychology of our times teaches us not to reject, in a body, facts which fall within human possibility, but rather to investigate them from the point of view of well-ascertained laws. If clairvoyance is a faculty of the soul, we may no longer simply consign prophets, oracles, and sybils to the domain of superstition. Divination has really been known and practised in temples of old, with fixed principles and a social and religious end in view. The comparative study of religions and esoteric traditions shows that these principles were the same everywhere, although their application may have varied infinitely. What has discredited the art of divination is that its corruption has given rise to the worst abuses, and that its glorious manifestations are possible only in beings of exceptional purity.

Divination, as practised at Delphi, was founded on the principles we have just set forth, the inner organization of the temple corresponded thereto.

As in the great temples of Egypt, it consisted of an art and a science. The art consisted in penetrating the far-away past and future by clairvoyance or prophetic ecstasy; the science, in calculating the future in accordance with the laws of universal evolution. Art and science checked one another. All I will say of this science, called genethlialogy by the ancients, and of which the astrology of the middle ages is only an imperfectly understood fragment, is that it took for granted the esoteric encyclopedia as applied to the future of peoples and individuals. Though very useful in showing the direction things were taking, it was always of very doubtful application. Only the very loftiest minds knew how to use it. Pythagoras had thoroughly mastered it in Egypt, but in Greece it was practised with a less thorough or clear understanding. On the other hand, clairvoyance and prophecy had made considerable progress.

It is well known that this art was practised in Delphi through the agency of women, both young and old. They were called Pythonesses, and played the passive *rôle* of clairvoyant somnambulists. Their oracles, often obscure, were interpreted, translated, and arranged by the priests in accordance with their own lights. Modern historians have seen in the institution of Delphi scarcely anything more than the exploitation of superstition by intelligent charlatans. Besides the assent, however, given by the whole of philosophic antiquity to the Delphic science of divination, several oracles related by Herodotus, such as those regarding Croesus and the battle of Salamis, speak in its favour. Doubtless their art had its beginning, its condition of prosperity, and its decay. Charlatanism and corruption exercised their demoralizing influence in the end, as we see in the case of king Cleomenes, who bribed the high priestess of Delphi to deprive Demaratus of his throne. Plutarch wrote a treatise inquiring into the reasons for the decline and extinction of the oracles; this degeneracy was felt to be a misfortune throughout all classes of antiquity. At first, divination was practised with a degree of religious sincerity and scientific thoroughness which raised it to the height of a real ministration. On the pediment of the temple could be read the inscription : " Know thyself," and another one above the entrance door : " Let no one enter here with impure hands." These words explained to all comers that earthly passions, falsehood and hypocrisy were not to pass the threshold of the sanctuary, that within, in awe-inspiring solemnity, reigned divine Truth.

Pythagoras reached Delphi only after having

visited all the temples of Greece. He had stayed
with Epimenides in the sanctuary of Idaean Jupiter;
he had been present at the Olympic games, and
presided over the mysteries of Eleusis, where the
hierophant had given up his place to him. Everywhere had he been received as a master, and now he
was expected at Delphi. Here the art of divination
was in a languishing condition, and Pythagoras
wished to restore its former prestige and might.
Accordingly he went there not so much to consult
Apollo as to enlighten his interpreters and revive
their enthusiasm and energy. Through them his
influence would mould the soul of Greece and
prepare a future for the land.

Fortunately he found in the temple a marvellous
instrument reserved for him, to all appearance, by
the hand of Providence.

Young Theoclea belonged to the college of the
priestesses of Apollo. She sprang from one of those
families in which the priestly dignity is hereditary.
Her childhood had been fed on the mighty impres-
sions imparted by the sanctuary, the ceremonies,
pæans, and *fêtes* of Pythian and Hyperborean
Apollo. Evidently she was one of those maidens
born with an instinctive abhorrence for the things
which attracted others. They love not Ceres and
fear Venus, for the heavy atmosphere of earth

troubles them, and the vague glimpse they have obtained of physical love seems to them the rape of the soul, the pollution of their undefiled, virginal being. On the other hand, they are strangely sensitive to mysterious currents, to astral influences. When the moon was shedding her soft beams on the sombre groves near the fountain of Castalia, Theoclea would see white forms gliding by. She heard voices in open daylight. On exposing herself to the rays of the rising sun, their vibration threw her into a kind of ecstasy, during which she heard the singing of invisible choirs. At the same time she was quite indifferent to popular superstition and idolatry; a feeling of horror overcame her at the sacrifices of animals. She spoke to no one regarding the apparitions which disturbed her sleep, feeling with clairvoyant instinct that the priests of Apollo were not in possession of that supreme light she needed. The latter, however, had fixed on her with the object of persuading her to become Pythoness. She felt herself attracted by a higher world to which she had not the key. What were these gods who manifested themselves to her in vibrations which troubled her being, and to whom she owed her inspiration? This she would know before giving herself up to them, for great souls need to see clearly even in abandoning themselves to divine powers.

With what a deep thrill, with how mysterious a presentiment the soul of Theoclea must have been stirred when she saw Pythagoras for the first time, and heard his eloquent voice resound among the columns of the sanctuary of Apollo! She felt the presence of the initiator for whom she was waiting, she recognized her master. She wished to know; knowledge would come by him; he would make this inner world speak, this world she bore within herself!—He, on his side, must have recognized in her, with sure and penetrating glance, the living, thrilling soul he was seeking, to become the interpreter of his thoughts in the temple and instil therein a new spirit. No sooner had their eyes met, their lips spoken, than an invisible chain bound the sage of Samos to the young priestess, who listened to him without a word, drinking in his utterances with eager, attentive eyes. Some one has said that a profound vibration enables poet and lyre to recognize one another as they approach. Thus did Pythagoras and Theoclea recognize one another.

At sunrise, Pythagoras had long conversations with the priests of Apollo, ordained saints and prophets. He requested that the young priestess should be received by them, so that he might initiate her into his secret teaching and prepare her for her mission. Accordingly she was permitted to follow the lessons given daily in the sanctuary by the master. Pythagoras was now in the prime of life. He wore a white robe, girdled in Egyptian fashion; a purple band was wrapped round his majestic brow. When he spoke, his grave, mild eyes were fastened on his interlocutor, enveloping him in a warm, tender light. The very atmosphere seemed to become lighter and electric with intelligence.

The conversations of the sage of Samos with the highest representatives of the Greek religion were of the utmost importance. It was not merely a question of divination and inspiration, the future of Greece and the destiny of the whole world were at stake. The knowledge, titles, and powers he had acquired in the temples of Memphis and Babylon gave him the greatest authority and influence. To those who inspired Greece he had the right to speak as a superior and a guide. This he did with all the eloquence of his genius and the enthusiasm of his mission. To enlighten their minds, he began by telling them of his youthful days, his struggles and Egyptian initiation. He spoke to them of Egypt, the mother of Greece, old as the world itself, immovable as a mummy, covered with hieroglyphs in the recesses of its pyramids, though possessing in its tombs the secrets of peoples, languages, and religions. Before their eyes he unfolded the mysteries of great Isis, goddess of earth and heaven, mother of gods and men; then, relating his trials and ordeals, he plunged them, with himself, into the light of Osiris. Afterwards came the turn of Babylon, of the Chaldaean magi, their occult sciences, and those deep solid temples where they call forth the living fire, the abode of demons and gods.

As she listened to Pythagoras, Theoclea passed through wonderful sensations. All he said was branded in letters of fire in her mind. These things appeared to her both marvellous and yet well known. Instead of hearing something new she seemed to be recalling what she had already learned. The master's words set her turning over the pages of the universe like those of a book. No longer did she see the gods in their human image, but in their essence, forming things and spirits. With them she flowed in space, rising and falling. At times there came the illusion that she no longer felt the limits of her body, and was fading away into infinity. Thus her imagination entered by degrees into the invisible world, and the former traces she found of it in her own soul told her that this was the true and only reality; the other was only apparent. She felt that her inner eyes would soon open and read the truth.

From these heights the master suddenly brought her back to earth by relating the misfortunes of

Egypt. After developing the greatness of Egyptian science, he showed how it was dying away under the Persian invasion. He depicted the horrible atrocities committed by Cambyses, the pillaged temples, the sacred books committed to the flames, the priests of Osiris killed or dispersed, the monster of Persian despotism collecting beneath his iron hand all the old barbaric tribes of Asia, the half-savage nomad races of India, and the centre of the continent, awaiting only a favourable opportunity to fall upon Europe. Yes, this ever-increasing cyclone must burst upon Greece as certainly as the thunderbolt, collecting in the sky, must flash forth from the cloud. Was divided Greece prepared to resist this terrible attack? She did not even suspect it. Nations cannot avoid their destinies, which the gods precipitate upon them, unless they are ever watchful. Had not Egypt, that wise nation of Hermes, crumbled to ruin after six thousand years of prosperity? Greece, alas! and beautiful Ionia will pass away even sooner! A time will come when the solar god will abandon this temple, when barbarian tribes will overthrow its very walls, and shepherds lead their flocks to pasture on the ruins of Delphi.

Before such sinister prophecies the countenance of Theoclea became transformed, assuming a terrified expression. She sank to the ground, and, with arms clasped round a column and eyes fixed as though plunged in thought, she resembled the genius of Grief weeping over the tomb of Greece.

"Those are secrets," continued Pythagoras, "which must be buried in the depths of the temples. The initiate attracts death or repels it at his pleasure. By forming the magic chain of wills, initiates in this way prolong the life of nations. It is for you to postpone the fatal hour, to cause Greece to shine in splendour and beam forth with the word of Apollo. Nations and peoples are what their gods make them, but the gods reveal themselves only to such as appeal to them. What is Apollo? The word of the one God manifesting himself eternally in the world. Truth is the soul of God, his body is the light. Only seers, sages, and prophets behold it; men see only its shadow. Legions of glorified spirits, whom we call heroes and demi-gods, inhabit this light in spheres beyond number. This is the real body of Apollo, the sun of initiates, without his rays nothing great is done on earth. As the magnet attracts iron, so by our thoughts, our prayers, and actions do we attract divine inspiration. It is for you to hand over to Greece the word of Apollo, and Greece shall be resplendent with immortal light!"

With such language Pythagoras succeeded in restoring to the priests of Delphi the consciousness of their mission. Theoclea drank in every word with silent, concentrated passion. She was visibly becoming transformed beneath the thought and will of the master as by a slow incantation. Standing in the midst of the astonished elders, she untied her raven-black locks and thrust them back from her head as though she felt flames of fire playing in and about them. Her eyes, transfigured and wide open, seemed to behold the solar and planetary gods in their radiant, glowing orbs.

One day she fell into a deep, lucid sleep. The five prophets surrounded her, but she remained insensible alike to their voice and touch. Pythagoras drew near and said: " Rise and go where my thought sends thee. For now thou art the Pythoness !"

On hearing the master's voice, a long vibrating thrill ran through the whole of her body and she rose to her feet. Her eyes were closed, but she saw from within.

" Where art thou ?" asked Pythagoras.

" I am ascending——ascending all the time."

" And now ?"

" I am bathing in the light of Orpheus."

" What seest thou in the future ?"

"Great wars——men of might—— Apollo returns to dwell in his sanctuary, and I shall be his voice——! But thou, his messenger, thou art about to leave me, alas! thou wilt bear the torch of his light into Italy."

Long did the seer speak, with closed eyes, in musical, panting, rhythmic voice; then suddenly, with a sob, she fell to the ground like one dead.

Thus did Pythagoras pour a pure, undefiled stream of knowledge into Theoclea's breast, tuning her like a lyre for divine inspiration. Once exalted to these heights she became his torch, thanks to which he was able to sound his own destiny, see into the possible future, and direct his path along the strandless zones of the invisible. Such a striking counter-verification of the truths he taught filled the priests with admiration, aroused their courage and revived their faith. The temple now possessed an inspired Pythoness, and priests initiated into the divine sciences and arts; Delphi could once again become a centre of life and action.

Pythagoras remained there for a whole year. It was only after imparting to the priests all the secrets of his doctrine, and preparing Theoclea for his ministry, that he took his departure for Greater Greece.

This is the end of this publication.

Any remaining blank pages are for our book binding requirements and are blank on purpose.

To search thousands of interesting publications like this one, please remember to visit our website at:

http://www.kessinger.net

Printed in the USA
CPSIA information can be obtained
at www.ICGtesting.com
LVHW081741270823
756436LV00007B/507